In My Village They Say....

The wisest book of African Proverbs

By Mansa Nyawira

Copyright 2018, Mansa Nyawira, all rights reserved.

No parts of this book may be reproduced in any form or by any electronic or mechanical means, including information storage and retrieval system, without permission in writing from the publisher. The only exception is by a reviewer, who may quote short excerpts in a published review.

Introduction

Embark on a captivating journey through the pages of this exquisite book, where the wisdom of Africa comes to life. Inspired by my interactions with exceptional individuals from across the continent, this compilation displays the ageless elegance of African proverbs. Handed down through generations, these treasured sayings hold profound insights and priceless teachings. Although I offer my interpretations of some proverbs, their meaning remains as limitless as your imagination allows. Explore, reflect, and embrace the wisdom within these pages as you uncover your connection to Africa's vibrant mosaic of knowledge.

- ❖ **Whoever befriends monkeys will never have his stick and shirt hung at the top of the tree.**

If you have powerful and influential friends in your circle, you will rarely or never face justice... maybe just a tap on the wrist.

- ❖ **That which discourages the raven, the vulture does not touch.**

Cowards do not face what scares the brave. They would rather wait to kick you when you are down.

- ❖ **The lions who move silently are the ones who eat meat.**

Not everybody needs to know your next moves or goals, move in silence, and surprise them.

- ❖ **Whoever marries a beautiful woman has the same problems as the person who cultivates maize on the roadside.**

We can all agree that if you walk around displaying your wealth, eventually you will attract problems.

- ❖ **If you want the rain, you must also accept the mud.**

If you want a beach body but you are not prepared to put in the work, do you really want it?

- ❖ **Do not allow what can devour you to lick you.**

Stay away from anything that can harm your life in danger. Sticking your whole hand in a lion's cage at the zoo to caress its back will make a great picture, but it doesn't mean you should do it.

- ❖ **The fish has faith in the water, but it is water that boils the fish.**

Betrayal can come from relatives, close friends, colleagues, and our spouse. Do not let this quote boost your trust issues.

- ❖ **You cannot become a master of something you have not studied.**

I doubt you would agree to be a passenger on a plane where the pilot acquired knowledge from watching Youtube videos. Then again context matters.

- ❖ **The buttocks may grow bigger, but they can never choke the anus.**

People who know their worth are never intimidated when they see other people around them becoming successful in life.

- ❖ **What an old man can see while lying down. A child even standing cannot see it.**

The more you live and experience, the more you see beyond what others miss.

❖ A downstream river does not return upstream.

Once you've hurt someone with words or actions, you can't take it back.

❖ Two mountains can never meet but people do meet.

This is often said to people who are trying to avoid you or claim to never have time to meet up.

❖ **It is out of respect that the elephant comes to destroy your field at night because if it comes during the day what is it you can do about it? Nothing!**

It is important to never confuse respect with fear, or one day end up in tears.

❖ **You must never remove your mother's panties from the clothesline even if it is raining.**

Keep your parent's personal affairs to yourself, even if you believe it will help them. Do not interfere or share them in public.

❖ **Mosquitoes do not like games where people clap too much.**

Not everyone who claps for your success and achievements in life is genuinely happy for you. Some are clapping but praying for you to fail.

❖ **The rooster that sings so proudly today must never forget that it came out of an egg.**

Never forget where you came from and those who made it possible for you to be where you are today.

❖ **It is the bananas that had agreed to be eaten raw, but the green plantains were violently opposed to that ridiculous idea.**

People will respect you according to how you want to be respected and how you carry yourself.

❖ **You only throw stones at the ripe mangoes.**

When you become successful at what you do. Jealousy, criticism, and attacks will find your address.

- ❖ **The Hawk wants the goat, but it does not have the strength to catch it.**

This is simply about having realistic goals in life.

- ❖ **A child on his mother's back will never stumble.**

Many mistakes in life can be prevented by following the guidance of those who are more experienced than us.

❖ **It is often the person for whom you went to fetch water in the river who excites the leopard against you.**

An ungrateful person will not hesitate to turn against you whenever an opportunity arises.

❖ **A falling tree makes more noise than a growing forest.**

Your mistakes will get more attention, but you must never forget how far you have come from where you began.

- ❖ **The knee will never wear the hat when the head is around.**

In simple English… stay in your lane.

- ❖ **In the eyes of every beetle mother, her cub is a gazelle.**

Children are special in their parent's eyes… generally speaking.

❖ **When it rains, the drops do not only fall on one roof.**

We all experience tough times, but how we deal with tough times separates us from the rest.

❖ **If an elder is showing you the moon by pointing his finger up, do not focus on the dirt on his finger.**

Do not let someone's past or physical appearance limit your perspective, they might have something valuable to offer.

- **Despite the goat's anger, the feast will still take place.**

Do not waste time on things you cannot change, it is better to focus on what you can change.

- **The elderly head is sometimes bent forward, but it does not mean they are stupid.**

Old age may curve the elderly back, but it does not curve their intelligence or their wisdom.

❖ **A fly without an adviser will follow the corpse into the grave.**

From time to time we all need that someone to save us from ourselves.

❖ **One finger cannot wash the face but ten fingers can wash the body.**

You can achieve some things by yourself, but it is nothing compared to what you can achieve with a talented team around you.

- **A fly knows it can land anywhere it wants… except on fire.**

Know your limit!

- **Even the fish that lives in water is always thirsty.**

In the context of modern society, I believe it is a supernatural gift to be able to say "I have enough," and be happy and grateful for what we have.

❖ **We can repair the holes in our clothes, but not the holes in our mouths.**

Words have power so be careful with the words you speak because they can cause irreparable damage.

❖ **If you promise a calabash, give a calabash.**

Our lives and our words are the only things of value we have left, therefore, if you make a promise. Please fulfil it.

- ❖ **The sun does not ignore a village because it is small.**

In this life, everyone deserves to be treated with respect and kindness. Regardless of their social status.

- ❖ **Sheep move together but they do not have the same price.**

Never compare yourself to other people around you because you do not have the same experiences or backgrounds. Know your worth!

❖ **Do not push with your feet the pirogue that brought you to the dock.**

Treat the people who helped you become who you are today with gratitude and respect.

❖ **A word is something that does not rot.**

Words have power so be careful of the words you speak. People never forget the negative things we say to them.

- ❖ **It is at the end of the old rope that you weave the new one.**

The new generation needs the experiences of the previous generation to build on.

- ❖ **Small hammer breaks big pebbles.**

Strength comes in different ways, shapes, and forms. Size doesn't always matter... well, don't quote me on that

❖ **Poop does not hurt but when you step on it, you limp.**

Avoid stepping into situations that can be avoided. Some things may seem harmless but can have serious consequences.

❖ **A crocodile can scare you in the river but do not allow the fish to make fun of you.**

Never allow people to discourage you when you make mistakes while trying to achieve your dream. They do not have your courage or strength, keep pushing!

❖ **Bad luck does not lean against the tree.**

Bad luck knocks at everybody's door because it has everybody's home and work addresses.

❖ **If the tilapia tells you that the Nile perch is sick you better believe it because they both live in water.**

If someone tells you their boss or work environment is toxic, believe them and do not apply there.

❖ **Hot water never forgets that it was once cold.**

Never forget where you come from and the people who helped you become who you are today.

❖ **A brand-new flute hurts the owner's mouth.**

Do not give up old friends just because you have new ones.

❖ **Even if the lion has lost weight, the monkey will never be able to carry his body.**

A king will always be a king, regardless of the circumstances.

❖ **A dog may have four legs but it cannot follow two paths at the same time.**

Focus on one thing and do it to the best of your abilities.

- **A problem without a solution is not a problem.**

For every problem we face in life, there is always a solution.

- **The baobab still exists today because it did not try to resist the winds.**

Do not waste time and energy trying to explain yourself to people who cannot stand you.

❖ **Nobody should expose a problem without first swallowing saliva.**

Think before speaking about anything.

❖ **Whoever wants coal, supports the smoke.**

Nothing comes for free. Do you want it? Work for it.

❖ **Pain is like rice in a basket but if every day we all take one grain. There will be no rice left in the basket.**

That's why we show up when people are going through tough times in life.

❖ **What you cannot boil, you can grill.**

There is always more than one solution to a problem.

- ❖ **Pepper burns but maggots live in it.**

Some people cannot imagine eating one meal a day, but there are people around us who chose to only eat one meal a day.

- ❖ **A grain of corn is always in the wrong in front of a chicken.**

That's why some superpowers have invaded and destroyed countries around the world based on lies.

❖ **A blender you've once used to blend chillies, the smell never goes away.**

Forgiving someone for the wrong they've done, does not mean forgetting what they've done.

❖ **A fish only follows the stream of the river.**

Some people are only moved by Self-interest.

- ❖ **Whoever has not yet descended from the top of the mountain must not laugh at a toothless person.**

Do not judge a person if you haven't walked a mile in their shoes.

- ❖ **The chief of the village never sees the devil.**

Parents should never pick sides when solving their children's disputes.

❖ **Death lies in the folds of our coats.**

Death can be found anywhere and can knock at our door at any time.

❖ **The lizard performs push-ups without thinking about developing big biceps.**

Doing good deeds for people can be its own reward, without expecting anything back.

- **Mankind created watches, but it is nature that keeps the time.**

We live on borrowed time so stop postponing your dreams. Start now!

- **If you are not beautiful or handsome, then you better learn how to dance.**

Worry not about things you cannot change. Focus on things you can change.

❖ **Everyone knows Jesus, but he doesn't pay bills around here.**

You are free to choose your religion but remember to make a living.

❖ **The acacia does not fall at the will of a starving goat that wants its fruits.**

We all want things in this life, but if we do nothing to acquire those things, then it's just a dream.

- ❖ **Even if the panther has lost weight, you cannot call it a cat.**

Respect people for who they are not for the titles they have or had.

- ❖ **When a mosquito land on your testicles, you understand that violence does not solve anything in life.**

My advice is to always choose diplomacy if you cannot match the power.

❖ **It is the rain that gradually falls that fills the river.**

Patience is the key to happiness.

❖ **A mouse would never pull a tiger's moustache.**

Reminds me of the person who stuck his finger in a lion's cage. I mean, what can I say? At least it went viral.

❖ **Whoever swallows a coconut must have faith in his anus.**

You must have confidence in self to accomplish anything you wish.

❖ **If you are peeling groundnuts for a blind man, you must always keep whistling so that he knows you are not eating them.**

Nothing builds trust and maintains strong relationships with others better than being accountable.

- ❖ **If you see a dark goat during the daytime catch it, because you might not find it during nighttime.**

When you see an opportunity, seize it, and do not let it go.

- ❖ **It is the bugs in your bed that will sting you.**

It is always the people closest to you who will stab you in the back.

❖ **One piece of wood gives the smoke but not the fire.**

Alone we can accomplish some things, but together we can accomplish anything.

❖ **You do not breed a dog on the day of the hunt.**

We've all at least once, procrastinated so much that we tried to prepare for an exam on the morning of that exam.

❖ **He who has not yet crossed the river must not make fun of someone who has drowned.**

Athletes always make sports look so easy that from the comfort of our couches, we believe we can do better.

❖ **The marks of the whip disappear, but the traces of insults never do.**

Once again remember words have power so use them wisely.

- ❖ **Money does not bury people the way people bury people.**

No amount of gold or jewels can match the priceless treasure of having people who love and care for you in this life.

- ❖ **The elephant cannot run and scratch his buttocks at the same time.**

Don't scatter your energy on many things, but concentrate on one thing and master it.

❖ **In a court of fowls, the cockroach never wins a case.**

Justice or fairness is a mirage for those who are oppressed or discriminated against by those in power.

❖ **A cow can shake its tail but the tail will never shake the cow.**

At your workplace, your employer can be fired, but you can never fire your employer.

- ❖ **If a person pretends to die, you also have to pretend to bury that person.**

Remember to match people's energy out there. Especially, if they are being disrespectful to you.

- ❖ **Whoever can put an egg in a bottle, can also remove it.**

If you can start a fight, you can also end it.

❖ **It takes a village to raise a child.**

A child's education is not solely the responsibility of the parents or family but also that of the community.

❖ **When a monkey wants to climb a tree, its butt must be clean.**

Make sure you are irreproachable before you judge someone else.

- ❖ **If you are not scared, you do not have courage.**

Courage is not the absence of fear, but rather the ability to act despite fear.

- ❖ **Whoever teases a wasp nest must know how to run very fast.**

Choose your battles carefully.

❖ **The one who follows the street named "I don't care" shall arrive at the village named "If I knew".**

One day, someday, eventually... you will regret it.

❖ **Stop chasing dogs out of wedding parties because you are all there for the same reason.**

Do not exclude people from events or gathering just because they are different.

❖ **When you cut the ears, the neck begins to worry.**

"Maybe I'm next"... That's how you feel when your employer begins sacking people.

❖ **The depth of the river is never measured with one finger.**

People shouldn't be judged based on one aspect of their lives. It will be not only unfair but also a disservice to who they truly are.

❖ **A united flock forces the lion to sleep hungry**

People who work together as a team can overcome any challenges.

❖ **The bottom of the pot does not fear fire.**

People who have faced challenging situations before are never afraid when it happens again. They've got the experience needed.

❖ **Wait to cross the river before saying that the crocodile is ugly.**

"If it were me I would've done it this way or that way" while sitting comfortably at home on the couch watching tv and judging a boxer being punched all over in the ring.

❖ **The boat leaves, but the port remains.**

After a breakup, life goes on. After an accident, life goes on. After a failed exam, life goes on. The situation does not matter, life still goes on.

- ❖ **Children are like clay, they will always take the shape they are given.**

Children are the products of the education they received at home and the environment they grow up in.

- ❖ **Black hens lay white eggs!**

Appearance can be misleading.

- **Silver coins make a lot of noise inside a pocket, but bills are silent.**

Sometimes people who make the most noise in the room are the most insecure, they are scared.

- **When two elephants fight, the grass suffers.**

When war is declared between two countries, it is also the civilians, people who are not involved in the dispute who suffer the most.

❖ **The youth can walk faster but the elder knows the road.**

The youths have more energy and enthusiasm, but older people possess wisdom and experience.

❖ **If you cannot climb some of the trees your ancestors climbed, at least put your hands on the trunk.**

If you cannot match your ancestors' achievements, at least follow their footsteps and learn from their experiences.

- ❖ **Elders keep themselves warm with the woods harvested in their youthful days.**

Invest and plan your future while you are still young.

- ❖ **The dog who belongs to the chief of the village is not the chief of dogs.**

It is not because you hang around powerful people that you are powerful. Humble yourself.

- **The hen is never ashamed of the henhouse.**

You should never be ashamed of where you came from.

- **It is better to sit on a stool that belongs to you than to sit on a chair you have borrowed.**

What's yours is yours, no matter how small it may be. Nobody can take that away from you. Be proud and happy that it is yours.

❖ **Never put your finger between the bark and the tree.**

One must never get involved in a dispute between a married couple. They know each other very well.

❖ **A shaman will always teach all the secrets to his children, but he will always keep one or two for himself just in case.**

Teaching is good but it is better to allow the student to put the theory in practice and learn from it.

- ❖ **It is better to look in front of you than to look back at the places where you once stumbled.**

Mistakes of the past are lessons we've already learned from, focus on the present and future not to miss the new lessons.

- ❖ **If the goat takes a few steps back, do not think it is cowardice.**

Do not judge people based on their first impressions or actions, they might surprise you.

- ❖ **Guinness pays to be advertised everywhere, but palm wine does not. However, they are both popular in Africa.**

When you know your worth there is no need to compare yourself to others.

- ❖ **The hidden snake grows.**

It is the small and unresolved problems that become big problems if they are not addressed.

❖ **A child can also play the drum and adults can dance because they taught the child how to play.**

Children learn from adults but sometimes adults can also learn a thing or two from children.

❖ **The fire that will burn you is the fire you use to keep warm.**

It is always the people who are the closest to us who hurt us the most.

❖ **It is not because of thirst that the crocodile leaves the lake in the morning to drink water from the dew that falls on the leaves.**

Sometimes people may do things we do not understand, but it doesn't means there isn't a logical reason.

❖ **An army of sheep led by a lion can defeat an army of lions led by a sheep.**

A great leader can have a significant impact on the outcome of a situation.

❖ **The mouse does not ride on the cat's back.**

It is important to recognise danger and avoid it whenever possible. Instead of shark diving, stay at home.

❖ **You cannot plough, sow, harvest, and eat on the same day.**

Trust the process, and be patient, it will eventually pay off.

❖ **The goat grazes where it is tied.**

When you find your calling or what you love doing in this life, study it, master it, sharpen your tools, and work smartly to be the best at it.

❖ **The sheep always keeps its head down because it is ashamed to see the goat's anus.**

In other words, humility is a virtue.

- ❖ **If you want milk from the lioness, you must be prepared to give it a piece of meat.**

Be prepared to pay the price or make sacrifices for whatever it is you want in life.

- ❖ **It is okay not to like cheetahs, but you cannot deny the fact that they are the fastest beast in the wild.**

Pay respect where respect is due.

- ❖ **The future embarrasses whoever does not know the past.**

Know your history!

- ❖ **While you are waiting for the mango to become ripe, your friends have already started eating it with a pinch of salt.**

Do not wait for the right time to start, start now!

❖ **It is the famine that made the village eat fruits from the strange trees.**

In other words, desperate times call for desperate measures.

❖ **By working together, the teeth can chew meats.**

We can achieve anything together.

- ❖ **When the monkey sees tasty fruits on a tree It cannot reach them. The monkey claims that those fruits are rotten.**

Be careful of people who try to discourage you from achieving your dreams just because they are unhappy with their outcomes.

- ❖ **A tree alone cannot withstand a storm.**

There is power and strength in unity.

❖ **Lies produce flowers but not fruits.**

The truth about any situation will always come out, no matter how long it takes.

❖ **The eagle may have flown very high in the skies, but its bones are always found on the ground.**

Death does not discriminate. Rich or poor, we will all be welcomed.

❖ **Whoever the snake has bitten in the past becomes wary of caterpillars.**

Traumatic experiences can easily make a person very cautious or fearful of anything that reminds them of it.

❖ **Whoever wants honey must have the courage to face the bees.**

Do you really want it? If yes, then go for it.

❖ **The hat receives the same honours as the head.**

A well-mannered child in public reflects the parents' or family's values.

❖ **A tree that has been struck by thunder is never afraid when the rainclouds turn dark.**

What doesn't kill you only makes you stronger.

❖ **The sheep's penis is eaten early in the morning.**

In other words, life belongs to those who wake up early.

❖ **To laugh at your neighbour's anus is not a crime. However, to invite your entire family to do so is unacceptable.**

It is unacceptable to laugh at someone in public for something they disclosed to you in private.

❖ **The leopard does not move without its spots.**

People's characters or nature cannot be changed, even if they try to hide or disguise it.

❖ **The fig never falls straight into our mouth.**

If you really want it, then you better get up and go get it.

- ❖ **If you see a snake on a bicycle, it means it has found a way of pedalling.**

This is a gentle reminder to remember to mind your own business.

- ❖ **If you behave like a crab, you will be eaten with noise.**

There will come a time when you will have to face the consequences of your actions.

❖ **The egg does not dance with the stone.**

Know your limits in life.

❖ **The forked tongue does more harm than the stumbling foot.**

My friend, you better watch what you say.

❖ **Be careful if you are teaching a parrot how to talk because one day it is going to verbally abuse you.**

Be careful what you teach or say to people, because one day they might use it against you.

❖ **The henhouse is a sumptuous palace for the rooster, despite the horrible smell of the place.**

Be grateful, happy and proud of what you have instead of moaning about what you don't have.

❖ **We are slow to grow, but we are quick to die.**

Let's make the most of life while we can still smell flowers.

❖ **Whoever learns without doing is ploughing without sowing.**

Knowledge is power, but if you are not using that knowledge, then it is useless.

- **If you are staring at an ugly picture, it is better to make sure that it is not your reflection.**

Some people should first look at themselves in the mirror before judging anyone.

- **Whoever is in a hurry to have a child will marry a pregnant woman.**

Patience is key.

❖ **The old man's mouth may be smelly, but very good advice can come out of it.**

Judging people based on how they look can make one miss an opportunity to learn.

❖ **If the tree knew, what the axe had in mind it would have never helped to make the handle.**

Sometimes, your kindness and generosity can be used against you.

- ❖ **Only death makes it possible for the mouse to dance on a cat's skin.**

When people no longer respect you, make sure you leave that space. However, if you choose to stay... get your clown costume ready.

- ❖ **Homeless people do not have the wealth of this world, but there is always someone mourning at their funeral.**

No further comment.

❖ **The Ox does not boast of its strength in front of the elephant.**

Be respectful and humble or life will humble you.

❖ **One hand alone cannot clap.**

Like Caesar once said, "Apes together strong".

- ❖ **You do not go to your neighbour's funeral to say, "My wife's coffin was better than your wife's coffin".**

Remember not to be rude, insensitive or disrespectful to someone who is grieving.

- ❖ **If your face turns to the sun, all shadows fall behind you.**

Never let problems overshadow your hopes or happiness. Focus on the positive aspects of your life.

❖ **Each river has its own source.**

It doesn't matter how many years of experience you have, do not be overconfident or careless.

❖ **The Mbuti people's shadow is always taller during sunset.**

Things come and go, but it must never change your attitude towards life.

❖ **If your brother is stubborn like a nail, you must hit harder.**

Be assertive and decisive when dealing with disrespectful or problematic people.

❖ **A man never goes far from where his corn is roasting.**

Stay consistent and show up every day for your dreams and goals.

❖ **You can start a war but there must be at least two people to make peace.**

I mean…

❖ **If you want your clothes to dry you must hang them where the sun is shining.**

If you want to grow you must expose yourself to opportunities.

❖ **A cup full of water is more valuable than a dried-up sea.**

What you can't change is not worth your worry, what you can change deserves your attention.

❖ **Powerful tools in the wrong hands can make sugar taste bitter.**

Leadership demands excellence, not everyone can rise to the challenge.

- ❖ In the elderly house, not everything is old.

- ❖ The man who has shit in the bush will forget, but the man who has stepped on the shit in the bush will never forget.

- ❖ Whoever sells eggs should never fight.

- ❖ When the cat was not hungry, it claimed that the mouse's behind was stinking.

- ❖ Money does not wash but it makes you clean.

- ❖ The ashes that were believed to be extinguished are the ones that burned the house.

- ❖ Life is a succession of happy moments and sudden misfortunes.

- ❖ A conversation is like a meal, anyone who is present can participate.

- ❖ Mosquitoes are dying because they think people are applauding for their singing talents.

- ❖ You can get paid to climb a coconut tree, but to come down from it is your choice.

- ❖ The roads that lead to friendship are never long.

- ❖ Elephants never complain about their tusks, but we all know it is a heavy burden to carry alone.

❖ Wisdom is a seed that is harvested from old people.

❖ Where the heart is, the feet never hesitate to go.

❖ The man who falls from a tree will get up. The man who falls from a horse will get up. However, the man who falls for a woman skirt will never get up.

- ❖ You never bring a knife to reconcile, but you bring a needle to sew

- ❖ A child can stare at the moon, but not the sun.

- ❖ The sigh of a beautiful woman is louder than the lion roar.

- ❖ Whoever wears borrowed clothes is actually naked.

- ❖ You can hide a fire, but you can never hide the smoke.

- ❖ If you kill goats, you will forget their faces. However, if you kill someone, you will never forget that person's face.

- ❖ If you seek what must not be sought, you shall find what you were not looking for.

- ❖ You cannot become the master of something you have not studied.

- ❖ Before you call someone ugly, you must remember that dirty water can stop a bushfire.

❖ It is not because there are no more dogs in the village that the hunter will put a bell on a cat to replace the dog.

❖ Too many praises make the cat think it is a lion.

❖ Pleasant words attract the snake out of its hole.

- ❖ If you slam your head against a jug and it sounds hollow, do not necessarily assume that it is the jug that is empty.

- ❖ If you see a turtle sitting on a wall, understand that it is there because someone put it there.

- ❖ The person who always asks for direction is a person who will never get lost.

❖ If you leave the forest at the same time as the buffalo, then you better know how to climb a tree.

❖ Even when dry, the river keeps its name.

❖ A well travelled young person is older than an elder who has never left the village.

- ❖ A person with diarrhoea is never afraid of darkness.

- ❖ If you want to improve your memory, then lend someone money.

- ❖ We see things better through the eyes that cried.

- ❖ The only thing stronger than elephants is a bush.

- ❖ A smile is a universal language.

- ❖ The Zebra's shadow has no stripes.

❖ Turtles do not give birth to hairy babies.

❖ If someone forgets you, you must forget them too. Nobody came to this earth to become someone else's memory card.

❖ Be careful of a patient person's silence.

❖ If you lick the lion's tongue, he will devour you.

❖ A flaw can fade, but it does not die.

❖ hen you walk away from a place in life, you must always remember to leave the door slightly open. It might get dark where you are going and you might need a little bit of light to help you move forward.

- ❖ The smartest students in the school of life are not the students who believe they know the answers. The smartest students are the ones who do not know the answers but raise their hands anyway. They are the ones who will always learn because they either get it right by luck and if they get it wrong they are taught the right answers by the school of life through experience.

- ❖ Knowledge without action is not power, but knowledge with action is power. If you want to achieve anything in this life. Please get up, and go for it!

The End...